HOW to LOSE IT

ANNA WILLIAMSON

MENTAL health SORTED

Thanks to my gorgeous niece and nephew, Maddie and Josh - such a wise pair, cheers guys - and the students of Freman College for letting me utilize their experience as 'consultants'.

And a massive thank you to the inspirational Liz Rowe and my mentor Floyd Waithaka for being my all-seeing and all-hearing guru to keep me on track.

Scholastic Children's Books,
Euston House, 24 Eversholt Street,
London NW1 1DB, UK

Scholastic Ireland,
89E Lagan Road, Dublin Industrial Estate,
Glasnevin, Dublin D11 HP5F

A division of Scholastic Ltd
London ~ New York ~ Toronto ~ Sydney ~ Auckland
Mexico City ~ New Delhi ~ Hong Kong

Published in the UK by Scholastic Ltd, 2019

ISBN 978 1407 19314 4

Printed in Italy

2 4 6 8 10 9 7 5 3

Papers used by Scholastic Children's Books are made from wood grown in sustainable forests.

www.scholastic.co.uk

CONTENTS

OKAY, LET'S GET OFF TO THE RIGHT START AND LEVEL WITH EACH OTHER SHALL WE...? I BET YOU'RE WONDERING IF THIS BOOK IS GOING TO BE ANY GOOD? IS IT GOING TO BE HELPFUL? PERHAPS YOU'RE A FAN OF READING, OR MAYBE, LIKE MY BROTHER, YOU'D MUCH RATHER TUNE INTO YOUTUBE (STUFFING YOUR FACE WITH CRISPS) THAN READ A BOOK... WELL, WHATEVER HAS PROMPTED YOU TO PICK UP THIS BOOK, I WANT TO SAY A MASSIVE WELCOME AND WELL DONE FOR DOING SOMETHING POSITIVE FOR YOU.

This book is all about the often tricky topic of mental and emotional health. I'm wondering what your thoughts are on mental health? Is it something you've heard much about? Perhaps you've heard people at school, family members, or on the TV talk about it? Or maybe you've got no idea. Whatever your thoughts and experiences so far, that's totally okay, because in this book we are going to explore some of the most common and sometimes confusing or scary aspects of our mental health. The head stuff. The 'what goes on in that weird and wonderful mind of ours' malarkey.

Before we get stuck in, I wanted to clear up any doubt or questions you might have about me. I think it's only right that if I'm going to be prying into your private thoughts, feeling and actions, then I tell you a bit about *me* in return... Sound fair?

I'm **ANNA**, I'm a TV and radio presenter, an author of books that help people, and I'm also a counsellor and life coach – someone who listens to people's worries and problems, and helps in working through them.

As a kids' TV presenter I would hear from young people all the time. They would tell me their problems and worries, and ask if I could help with advice. So, I decided to join the children's helpline, Childline, a charity where anyone under the age of 19 can call, email or message in for free, at any time of the day or night, and speak to a trained counsellor privately.

A few years ago, when I wasn't that much older than you, I suffered with mental health issues. At the time I was pretty scared as I was thinking and feeling all sorts of weird things in my head and body, and I didn't know what to do about it, or if I should tell someone. I was having a pretty stressful time and eventually, because I'd been keeping all my worries in, they all came spilling out one day (with lots of tears) to a friend at work, and then my mum, and finally I got some help.

I was so impressed with telling a trained therapist about how I was feeling, and learning and working out how I could look after my mental health better, that I decided to learn all about it myself. I'm now a trained therapist myself, helping other people who might need it if things get a bit stressful, confusing....and well, downright rubbish in life.

- Don't be scared. Think of anxiety as your friend – it's your body's way of protecting you.
- Panicky, anxious feelings WILL go away. Take slow, deep breaths and let those feelings run out of steam.
- Tell a friend – you can feel so much better by sharing your feelings with someone you trust.

First up, let's understand what we mean by 'mental health'. The official (and rather stuffy) definition is *'a person's condition with regard to their psychological and emotional wellbeing'*. In the real world that basically means everything about us that isn't part of our physical health. So, our thoughts, feelings, emotions and behaviours... I'm sure you'll agree that's a pretty massive part of who we are. And yet for a long time there has been an attitude that mental health is something to be embarrassed, even ashamed, about. Let me tell you now: that is **NOT TRUE!**

Let's be clear – there are many different potential mental health issues, some trickier than others. And for people who are suffering with serious mental health illnesses, they can be treated and cared for in appropriate places.

But remember – mental health is something we have **every day!** So, we need to take care of it. Just as we look after our physical health by eating, drinking and sleeping properly, we also need to fuel our mental health. Good food, plenty of water and proper rest is super important for our mental health, too. And there are other things we can do, such as sharing worries, making sure we keep stress levels low and enjoying some proper downtime.

Mental health is **everyone's** business. We all have times when we feel stressed, sad, worried or frightened, and most of the time those feelings pass. But sometimes they can develop into a more serious problem – and it could happen to any one of us. Your mental health doesn't always stay the same – it can change as you move through different stages of life.

We are all individuals and experience things differently – what one person bounces back from quickly might weigh another down. Never judge someone else by their ability to cope with mental health challenges – after all, we are all brilliantly unique.

MYTH BUSTING

....

'People with mental health problems are weak.'

BUSTED!

We *all* have mental health. Sometimes we get a cough and cold and we have to visit the doctor for some help. Well, it can be the same for mental illness – sometimes people feel so sad that they can't get out of bed or they feel too scared to go to certain places. So, they might need to see a doctor for some help. Nobody is ever weak for asking for help with either a physical or mental health problem. In fact, it shows how strong and brave you are.

'Boys don't suffer with mental health issues as much as girls.'

BUSTED!

Er, hello?! Boys are human beings too, right? Boys are just as likely to suffer with mental health problems as girls. They just don't tend to talk about it as much.

WHAT ARE THESE FUNNY
FEELINGS?

Do you ever get those moments when your hands feel all sweaty and you get a bit dizzy and 'weird', and you want to run away to anywhere else, perhaps even suddenly needing the loo?

You know – like when you're about to start a school test ... or walk into a friend's birthday party by yourself ... or when your teacher asks you a question in front of the **WHOLE** class and all you want to do is let the ground swallow you up as your heart beats like crazy and you go bright red in the face...

Well, you might be surprised to know that **MILLIONS** of people feel the same. One in six young people, to be exact – that's around five in your classroom. It means you're completely and utterly normal. Yep, experiencing feelings like these (and there are lots more, too) are all signs of 'anxiety' – and guess what, we ALL have the anxiety trigger buried away in our brains. It's actually a good thing, and something that dates back to our **cavepeople ancestors**

– something we all need to keep us safe. The annoying thing about anxiety though, is that it often doesn't *feel* so good. It can make us feel scared, worried, lonely – and a bit freaked out.

I know how anxiety can feel – it can suck big time. But like a lot of things in life, the more we learn about WHY it happens and what we can do about it, the better we can feel. Then hopefully we can stop it from happening in the first place, or learn how to make it go away when we don't need it.

Are you ready to become the boss of anxiety? Let's get to the nitty-gritty!

HEADS-UP!

What is anxiety?
- A general feeling of worry that something bad is going to happen.
- Feeling nervous or uneasy about something with an uncertain outcome.

The LOWDOWN

Back in prehistoric times there were threats around every corner – rival tribes, sabre-toothed tigers... Thankfully, everyone had (and still has now!) an in-built panic alarm, which would go off whenever a threat appeared. You might have heard of it before – the 'fight-or-flight response'. It basically means that as the stress hormone (adrenaline) is naturally triggered in the brain, it rushes through the body, and you either fight off the attack or you get the heck outta there!

ANXIET-REX

You know that sudden rush of nervous energy you get before running a school race, or the extra fizz of focus you get when taking an exam? That's caused by adrenaline, too. This, my friend, is good old anxiety doing its thing. And when it's doing its job in this low-key way, anxiety is a good thing.

It's when we start to feel anxious at times and in situations where we don't need it, or it starts to bubble up to the surface, that anxiety becomes an unwelcome challenge.

WHEN ANXIETY TURNS BAD

The nifty fight-or-flight alarm hits a snag in the modern world. We no longer live like cavepeople with the same intense threats – but as the human race has evolved, our anxiety response has stayed in prehistoric times.

Life has a habit of throwing us challenges, often when we could do without them. School niggles, exam pressure, relationship stress – these are all things that can test our feelings and emotions.

If we don't let the heat of stress or worrying thoughts out, they stay trapped inside our heads and fizz and fizz until eventually they find an exit. A lot of people have anxiety or panic attacks – a temporary strong reaction to a built-up feeling of stress and worry. These attacks are basically the fight-or-flight response going off like mad – but we don't need such a massive and often scary reaction to anxious feelings.

Imagine the anxiety trigger inside your head is like a tightrope. A healthy setting for your response to an anxious situation is for the rope to be pretty slack and loose – you know, like it would take an elephant to run into it at full pelt to make it go taut and set off the trigger.

Now imagine that over time things have been happening in your life, which have been slowly increasing your stress and worry levels, and at the same time, the tightrope has wound up tighter and tighter … until it's at the point it's rigid, so all it takes is a mere flick for the rope to react and the trigger to go off. This is what happens when your stress and worries stay trapped in your head – and this is called an anxiety or panic attack.

HOW ANXIETY CAN AFFECT YOUR BODY...

- cold/hot sensations
- sweaty
- dizzy or light-headed
- blushing
- feeling faint
- heart beating fast
- struggling to breathe
- needing the loo
- feeling sick
- dry mouth

WHEN ANXIETY ATTACKS!

So, I think we're all agreed that anxiety can feel pretty awful. We get that it's there to protect us, but that doesn't make it feel any less horrible. There are all kinds of reasons why we might feel anxious, and the really annoying and confusing part of it is that it often doesn't make sense why it happens at certain times.

A big part of this is that life changes, and stuff happens. School stuff, family stuff, friend stuff... Upsetting things happen such as someone we care about gets ill or dies or leaves, or we feel embarrassed or scared in a strange or new place or situation, or we hear or see upsetting things on the news. Have a think now about a time when things in your life might have suddenly changed, or something has worried you.

Did you know how to deal with it?

All of the situations above are perfectly normal and reasonable times for someone to feel anxious. Sometimes it can feel as though you're the only one struggling or having horrible symptoms. But, you are not alone! In your school, there will be a huge number of others who also have moments of anxiety. Mental health is invisible in many ways, so we can't see when someone else might be struggling – but even though we can't see it, it doesn't make it any less terrible to suffer. So, next time you think you're the only one, remember – you're totally not! There are millions of people all signed up to the anxiety club.

HOW TO NOTICE ANXIETY:

- FINDING IT HARD TO CONCENTRATE
- NOT EATING PROPERLY
- TROUBLE SLEEPING
- WORRYING ALL THE TIME
- FEELING TEARFUL OR CRYING
- BEING CLINGY
- FEELING UNSETTLED AND TENSE
- THINKING YOU'RE UNWELL, SUCH AS A HEADACHE OR TUMMY ACHE
- FEELING ANGRY OR IRRITABLE

How to Kick a PaNiC ATTaCk in the BUTT

Now you know what panic attacks are, I'm going to help you become the boss of them.

The first thing to remember is that you will never die from a panic attack – you can feel pretty rubbish for the few minutes the attack is happening, but it won't harm you and you **WILL** feel better once it's gone.

Ready to kick the attack in the butt?

If you feel the first niggles of a panic attack creeping on – maybe a flutter in your tummy, feeling hot, dizzy, breathless, or maybe feeling a bit sick.

Get yourself into a safe space. If you're at school, find a quiet corner and ask a trusted friend to sit with you.

Sit down as comfortably as you can and get that breathing under control. When we feel panicky our breathing can get really fast and we don't actually breathe in and out properly – which can make us feel worse.

In your own time, sit up nice and tall. Close your eyes if you feel you want to, and breathe in through your nose for seven seconds, then out through your mouth for eleven seconds. Imagine you're blowing out a birthday-cake candle, really, really slowly.

If you feel a 'rush' or 'whoosh' of anxiety as the attack peaks (a bit like getting to the top of a rollercoaster before it whizzes down), just allow the feeling to happen. Let it ease off as it runs out of steam – and it WILL ease off, I promise. The more we try to stop the panic, the more it will try to happen – so let it do its thing. It won't last.

Remind yourself that you are safe. Notice where you are to reassure yourself that you are fine and nothing can harm you.

Once the pesky panic attack has gone, you might feel tired and need a drink – this is because the adrenaline that helps a panic attack take hold has now gone and it can leave you feeling a bit wiped out.

Tell yourself: 'Well done! I got through that and I am safe and well.'

Try to tell a teacher, parent or trusted adult about what happened and how you felt, so they can give you a big hug and some well-deserved TLC.

Remind yourself that **YOU** are in control of a panic attack, not the other way around. That way it won't scare you in the future.

Ask Anna

Dear Anna,

Every time my teacher asks me a question in class I go bright red, my hands get all sweaty and my mouth just seems to stop working and I can't get the words out. It's so embarrassing. Why does this happen and what can I do about it?
Sadie, age 9

Anna says:

So many of us feel nervous and put on the spot when someone talks to us and/or asks a question. It can feel as though everyone is looking and that can cause feelings of sudden anxiety, which can come out in various ways such as blushing, feeling sweaty, your mouth going dry...

The main thing to remember is that you are completely normal and pretty much everyone knows what it's like to feel like this. Perhaps have a little chat with your teacher before or after class, explain how you're feeling and come up with a plan together to help you not feel so 'put on the spot'. I'm hoping your teacher will listen. If and when you're next asked a question in class, take a slow deep breath to keep calm and focus on the teacher – not looking at others can help to keep your mind on what you're doing. And if you don't know the answer, that's absolutely fine. Don't be afraid to say so! You won't be the only one and you don't have to be perfect all the time – nobody is.

How to Make Anxiety Chill Out

Anxiety isn't always a full-blown panic attack – it can come and go. We can live happily with anxiety as long as we have a few tricks up our sleeves to keep any unwanted 'bad' anxiety at bay. Try these tips to start building up your own anxiety-busting toolkit:

Who can you trust? Find someone you can talk to when you have any worries on your mind. Is it a family member, a schoolteacher, a friend's mum? Choose someone you feel comfortable with and have their number saved in your phone as a Favourite.

Why not go one step further and get a whole team of people you trust on hand, should you ever need them? Hold a hand out and identify one person for each of your five fingers. That way you have some pretty sweet back-up.

 If you struggle to talk to people, that's okay. Have a think about sending a text or email to that trusted adult. Writing stuff down can feel a lot easier.

 Try writing any worries or thoughts down on a piece of paper – yep, with an actual pen! It can be really helpful to brain-dump anything on your mind onto paper.

 Why don't you give that piece of paper to someone you trust to read? Or how about screwing it up and chucking it in the bin to represent that all those negative thoughts have gone out with the rubbish?

Anxiety: Sorted.

To Sum It All Up...

Essentially, it's about getting the worries and thoughts that are bothering you out of your head. Whether you talk, write or even sing about them (seriously – it works for Ed Sheeran!), it's amazing how getting your troubles out can kick anxiety in the butt.

The Lowdown on Feeling Down

Two

- Say 'yes' instead of 'no'! The best way to kick low mood and depression to the kerb is to take positive steps forward.
- Take note of any negative or worrying thoughts and challenge them with positive ones.
- Don't hide away and avoid people – it will make any rubbish feelings feel worse.

OMG I'M SOOOO DEPRESSED...

Okay, hands up! How many of us have at some point in our life declared 'OMG, I'm soooo depressed', when in fact we're just a bit miffed about something? I'll admit it, when I was younger I used to pipe up with this when

I'd had a bad day, if someone had annoyed me or my parents had made what I considered a rubbish decision (like deciding I wasn't allowed to go clubbing with my mates when I was fifteen – to be fair, they probably *did* have a point). But then, a few years later when I actually *did* have depression, I really tried hard to understand what it was all about.

So, how does it start? What does it feel like? What's the difference between low mood and depression? All great questions – let's do some digging.

MYTH BUSTING

'Isn't depression just feeling a bit sad?'

BUSTED!

Feeling sad is part of feeling depressed. But it's a different type of sadness to a 'healthy' type of sad over something such as missing a mate when they've gone away. Depression can feel like you're always bogged down with negative thoughts, without much energy or motivation.

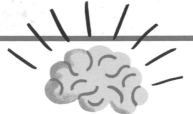

HEADS-UP!

Low mood and depression can feel like…

- sadness that doesn't go away.
- being grumpy or irritable a lot of the time.
- not being interested in things you used to enjoy.
- being tired or exhausted most of the time.

LOW MOOD vs DEPRESSION

One of the trickiest mental health illnesses to describe and to spot is depression. You may have heard of it before on TV, in the news or from others talking about it. It's fair to say, though, that most people are still confused about what depression actually is and why it happens. When we don't understand something, it can make it harder to deal with and if we don't do something about it, it can get worse. The easiest way to describe the difference between low mood and depression is to think of low mood as the warm-up act. Low mood can feel similar to feelings of depression, such as sadness, worrying thoughts, anxiety, tiredness, low self-esteem, frustration and anger.

But unlike the slightly more serious 'depression', low mood tends to lift after a few days or weeks.

It's important to remember that depression isn't simply someone being 'a bit sad or miserable'. One of the most unhelpful things you can say to someone who is feeling depressed is 'cheer up' or 'pull yourself together'. Believe me, they would if they could – no one chooses to have low mood or to be depressed. Who would, right? It's just not as simple as plastering a smile on your face and being all

'happy happy'.

But, there are a few quick fixes for 'catching' low mood before it sneaks into depression. These are some things that can usually resolve feelings of low mood: getting more sleep; eating healthy, regular meals; taking some time out; confronting any worrying or upsetting situations; talking about any problems with someone you trust. These tactics can take your low feelings and 'nip them in the bud' as my Nan used to say – and it's pretty spot-on advice.

If, after a few weeks, the low feelings don't improve, or perhaps are even worse, it's possible that depression has decided to pay a visit. So, it's important not to ignore any negative feelings – don't keep them bottled up, hoping they might go away. Going to the doctor can be pretty scary, but doctors are there to help (see page 170 for more on visiting your doctor).

HEADS-UP!

Depression – what to watch out for:

- trouble sleeping or wanting to sleep too much
- difficulty concentrating
- not wanting to hang out with friends or family
- unable to make decisions
- not feeling very confident
- eating less, or much more, than usual
- struggling to chill out
- feeling guilty (and not sure why)
- thoughts of suicide or self-harm
- feeling empty or 'numb' (unable to feel emotions)
- self-harm

WHY ME?

It can seem really unfair that some people experience mental health illnesses and others don't. Remember that mental health is something we ALL have, just like physical health. And, really, it makes sense that sometimes things happen that might make us feel unwell. When we feel poorly physically, we rest and take medicine. When worrying or upsetting things happen, our mental health needs extra love and attention, too.

Some studies by medical professionals say that depression affects almost one in four young people under the age of nineteen. It doesn't matter if you're white, black, green, red or covered in polka dots – anyone can feel unwell, mentally and physically, and there shouldn't be any embarrassment or weirdness around either.

Adults experience depression, too, but the scary reality is that first-time depression is happening in more young people than ever before. Now, I want to reassure you – this doesn't mean you're going to get depressed! But it can be really helpful to know why it happens, and recognize any signs in yourself or in others – just in case you can nip it in the bud.

● ●

Ask Anna

Dear Anna,

I used to play football and go to friends' houses after school, but now I just stay at home in my room. I feel angry and tired all the time and my teachers keep giving me grief as my homework is never in on time. I just can't be bothered. My parents spilt up last year and it was a really horrible time. I just don't really enjoy anything much any more, not even parties.
Aidan, age 14

Anna says:

It sounds like it's been a tough time for you. Parents breaking up almost always causes feelings of upset, which can make you feel tired, sad and angry. Our body and mind's way of processing and dealing with an upsetting event might be to shut down some of our emotions for a bit. This can make us feel a bit 'numb' and 'can't be bothered' about things we might have cared for before.

It's important you don't let this low mood get any worse. Have a think about who you could talk to about how you're feeling. How about an auntie, uncle or grandparent? It would also be worth having a chat with your parents, too, one at a time if it's easier, to tell them how upset you have been about their split. Their comfort and support should hopefully help in getting all that negative stuff out of your head, and help in getting you back to doing what you (used to) enjoy.

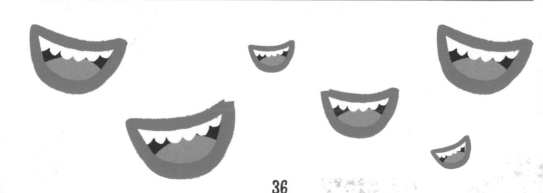

HOW TO CHECK YOUR MOOD

Worrying about things and having off days is perfectly normal. It's important that you don't diagnose yourself with something that you think is happening. Instead, go with the flow, check in with yourself and ask yourself questions to work out if what you're feeling is just a blip, or if it's something worth getting more support for.

Have a go at rating the following statements – you can just write on this page, or scribble down in a notepad or use your phone. Answer each statement for how you feel today – not yesterday or last week, but right now. Rate yourself on how happy you're feeling about each particular thing: 1 = No way! 10 = Yes, definitely!

I am looking forward to today. ☐

I want to hang out with my mates. ☐

School is going well for me. ☐

My home life makes me feel secure and happy. ☐

I am feeling satisfied with life. ☐

I sleep well. ☐

I'm eating a healthy, regular diet. ☐

I feel confident. ☐

I like myself. ☐

I can concentrate easily. ☐

Now, look at your results. Keep checking in with yourself regularly, rating the statements every day or each week or month, whatever feels right for you. If you're above 5 for most of them, great. If you're in the 8s, 9s and 10s, that's fantastic! If you're under 5 and creeping towards a 1 or 2 on any, it's definitely a good idea to share with a trusted adult, just to check nothing more troubling is going on.

SHUT UP DEPRESSION, YOU'RE A LIAR!

Childhood depression is different from the 'feeling cheesed off' everyday emotions. Feeling sad doesn't mean you're depressed – but if the feelings do carry on and start to interfere with social activities, hobbies, schoolwork or family life, it could mean that a depressive illness has sneaked in. It should be taken very seriously, but the good news is that there's lots that can be done to conquer it.

So, why might someone get depressed and how can it feel? Here are some examples:

'It can feel like nothing is going wrong, but at the same time everything is going wrong, and you aren't sure why. All you can constantly think about is the same things over and over ... there is nothing going on, it's just your brain.'
Zoe, 11

'Depression is a feeling of drowning while everyone around you is breathing; it can feel like you're trapped in your own mind with no escape. Depression gives you thoughts like "I'll never feel happy" or "I want to kill myself". SHUT UP depression, you're a liar!' James, 13

THINGS THAT CAN INCREASE THE RISK OF DEPRESSION:

- family problems
- school pressures
- friendship issues
- loss or death
- bullying

- physical, emotional or sexual abuse
- a family history of depression or other mental health issues

---

It can sometimes be just one thing that causes depression to set in or it can be a combination of things, too. All the things in the list above can take a toll on your mental health – it doesn't mean you're weak, it just means you're human!

One thing I want to make clear – like all mental health illnesses, depression is treatable. Of course, everyone responds differently to certain types of treatment, and whether it's medication or talking therapy (or both), there are options available to suit everybody (check out Chapter 8 for more on this).

MYTH BUSTING

'Boys with depression behave differently to girls with depression.'

BUSTED!

Depression is more common in girls than boys. With girls it tends to come and go, but with boys it's often more persistent and they are more likely to experience drug abuse and thoughts of suicide. Boys can sometimes be more aggressive and angry as a way of dealing with their depression.

Ask Anna

Dear Anna,

My friend is depressed. I try to cheer her up by taking her to places, but she just goes back to being sad again afterwards. She brings me down too when she's depressed. I don't know what to do.
Emily, age 13

Anna says:

It sounds like you're a great friend. As fab as it is to support your pal, it's also important to look after your own mental and emotional health. Keep supporting your friend by suggesting things to do together – maybe you could ask her what she'd like to do so she feels good about making positive decisions. And keep it chilled, too – like a movie on the sofa with loads of popcorn and snacks. But also make sure you spend plenty of time outside of the friendship doing things you enjoy, and seeing other friends who make you feel good about yourself. Being a friend to someone with depression can be difficult at times, but keep suggesting they get help and always put your own health first – after all, you can't be the best pal if you aren't feeling the best yourself.

DiD YOU KNOW?

Anyone can have a tough time and feel mentally unwell at times – these famous faces have all experienced depression:

CARA DELEVIGNE

LADY GAGA

JIM CARREY

DEMI LOVATO

J. K. ROWLING

CHANNING TATUM

HOW

DEPRESSION

WORKS

There is often a pattern to how low mood and depression sets in. Imagine it a bit like a five-person relay race – once each stage has run its course, the next one takes the baton to carry on towards the finish line.

People, places and events upset you – such as parents arguing, exam stress, bullying.

Thinking lots and worrying, with unhelpful thoughts whirling around your head – such as, 'I shouldn't feel like this', 'I'm hopeless and worthless', 'What if people are thinking bad things about me?'

Thoughts affecting your feelings and emotions – for example, 'I'm not much fun to be around' turns into feelings of guilt, worthlessness and sadness.

Feelings and emotions affecting how you look and behave – such as starting to sleep more than usual, feeling tired, lack of appetite, not bothering with personal appearance.

5 The vicious circle: the worse you feel, the less you do – the less you do, the worse you feel. You might comfort eat, stop seeing friends or start drinking alcohol or taking drugs.

Ask Anna

Dear Anna,

My mum has had depression for years. Does that mean I will get it?
Ella, age 13

Anna says:

Just because depression can be passed down in our genes, it certainly doesn't mean that we *will* get it. In fact, you may never experience depression at all.

Have a chat with your mum. Explain your worries and ask her how depression feels for her. Keep the conversation going and work out what you might do if you were to feel any low mood creeping in at any point in your life. By learning about it now and chatting about it in a relaxed way, you're in a really empowered position to spot any warning signs and to sort your mental health.

How to Boss Depression

There are lots of things to do to try and get out of the vicious circle of low mood and depression. The hardest thing is to actually 'do something' about it. But as difficult as it can feel to get the energy up, if you make a change in one area, the other areas can improve, too.

If you start to feel low, try this activity to see if it helps:

 Think about what's going in your life – have there been any changes, any worrying thoughts or behaviours (like staying in too much, harming yourself or having upsetting thoughts)? Be honest and think of a trusted adult you could talk to for support.

Get a routine going. Make sure you get up each day at a reasonable time and go to bed at a similar time each day, too. Add in eating regularly. This will give some structure to your day, which is really helpful in boosting your mood and not giving in to the rubbish feelings.

 Make activities and goals small, realistic and achievable. It might be as simple as going for a walk around the garden each morning – exercise really helps to boost mood.

 Say 'yes' instead of 'no'! When we're depressed it feels so much easier to just not bother with anything. This isn't helpful though – avoiding stuff and pushing people away only lowers your confidence more. So, be brave and say 'yes' to that invite!

Depression: Sorted.

To Sum It All Up...

Positive changes and baby steps forward are the best way to help boost your mood and kick depression in the butt. It might feel a bit scary, but you can totally do it!

Three

- To avoid worries and stress building up, try to plan everything in advance as much as you can.

- Stress can feel like pressure building up inside you, like you're about to pop. Try to calm down by doing something that makes you feel good.

- Take pressure and expectation off yourself and create realistic personal goals – instead of feeling like you have to sprint to the finish line, try to walk there first.

Worry often comes before stress and anxiety. It's important to recognize and deal with it early on so it doesn't turn into something bigger. Being able to manage worry when it first strikes will help you **be a worry warrior, not a worrywart.**

STRESS
sucks! sucks!

Any adult that says **'What have kids got to be stressed about?'** needs to spend a day in the life of a young person. There are things that are similar to what your parents experienced as children, such as friendship ups and downs and needing to do well at school, but the fact is there is so much more involved in being a young person today. The online world, increased school and social pressure, and the general pace of life have all ramped up, big time!

So, what is stress? And who might get it? Well, the answer to the second question is anybody. Just like the other mental health issues we're learning about in this book, stress doesn't pick and choose who to bother. We're starting to see a link here, huh? **Mental health affects us all.**

Let's shed some light on what stress is. Basically, it's a reaction to a pressure or threat. When we feel stressed, we feel tense, worried, nervous and 'on edge'. You know that hormone – adrenaline – that we talked about in the anxiety chapter? Well, this is also what is whizzing around your body causing some of those **funny stress feelings** – sweaty hands, your heartbeat or breathing getting faster, your legs feeling shaky...

Everybody feels stress at some time – it's a normal reaction to coping with certain situations. Some common causes of stress are:

- moving house or school
- a family breakup
- a life change, such as a different routine, a new teacher or a friend moving away
- a feeling of pressure coming from an area of your life
- 'people pleasing' – saying 'yes' so much that it makes you feel bad
- worrying about world issues such as terrorism and war

In an ideal world, stress comes and goes quickly, giving your mind and body a chance to rest. But there are some situations in life where stress can keep bubbling away, making everything hard to cope with. Finding and practising ways of coping with tricky situations can help to make sure that stress doesn't carry on, or even happen at all.

HEADS-UP!

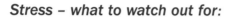

Stress – what to watch out for:

- changes in sleep patterns
- mood swings
- stomach aches and headaches
- changes in appetite – eating more or eating less
- trouble concentrating or finishing school work
- big changes in school performance
- lying
- bullying

And it can make you feel…

- Worried
- Tired – trouble getting to or staying asleep ('insomnia')
- Unable to relax
- Clingy to your parents or caregivers
- Like you want to spend time alone

This is one of my favourite **stress-busting activities**. When you've worked out the reason for your worry, you can start to do something about it – **simple.**

Grab yourself a piece of paper or use a drawing app on your tablet or phone. Draw a circle. Split it into eight equal parts so it looks like a cake you've cut.

- Label each part with something from your life, such as: family, home life, friends, school, social life, hobbies, online life and relationships.

- Rate each of these parts of your life out of 10 with the same question for each: how stressed am I about this? So, 1 = super chilled and 10 = super stressed.

Once you've written down your scores, have a look at how the Stress-O-Meter looks. The areas with the highest score are the ones causing you the most stress.

Ask yourself: '**What is it about this part of my life that is making me stressed, and what can I change?**'

Perhaps share your Stress-O-Meter with a trusted adult. It can help give them an idea of what life is like for you and any areas you need support with.

Try to make changes in your life to keep stress as low as possible – keep an eye any telltale feelings, don't load yourself up with too much and make sure you **plan in plenty of downtime to embrace boredom!**

Here's an example
of how your
Stress-O-Meter
could look:

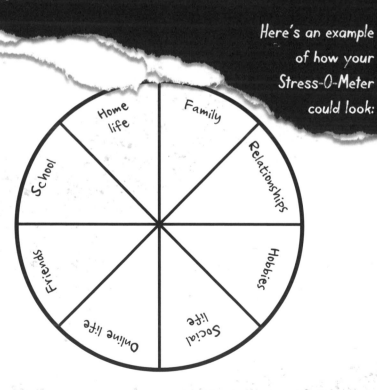

Home life

Family

Relationships

School

Friends

Hobbies

Online life

Social life

ANNOYING ADULTS!

It's pretty safe to say that parents and caregivers can get flipping annoying at times! Most of the time they mean well, but there are times when, like with any relationship,

ADULTS CAN BE A PAIN.

Cam, aged ten, sums it up well:

'My mum is seriously getting on my nerves! I get super mad at her – I just can't help it! Literally, the tiniest thing she does sets me off! She is sooooooo annoying!'

Hands up – who has ever felt the same?

There are so many reasons why our adults might get on our nerves and cause feelings of stress. Maybe they're always on your case to tidy your room; perhaps they don't let you go out with certain mates – or on the flip side, maybe they don't care where you go or who with. If your parents are together, there might be issues with their relationship, which can stress you out, or you might be having problems with other family members.

Without a doubt the biggest **parent problem** seems to be when it comes to school, exams and deciding on your future. Coping with pushy parents and trying to live up to their expectations is something many young people struggle with.

'My mum keeps comparing me to a friend from primary school who studies and works every day, and is one of those outstanding students. She's like, "Oh he's amazing, you should be like that." When I do try to study she's constantly making comments like, "You aren't properly studying" and "Where's your text book?" (when I don't have one for some subjects). It's making me feel like I want to scream and run away.'
Asif, 15

Parents can be **hard work** and often their love and worry can come across as anything but. We can't change how someone else thinks and talks to us, but we can be in control of our own thoughts. If your mum, dad or caregiver is saying things that are stressing you out, try to keep calm and tell them how it's making you feel. As crazy as it sounds, they might not even realize how badly their behaviour is affecting you. They aren't mind readers! You could write down your thoughts and feelings in a letter and give it to them – that way you can make sure everything you want to say has been said. (See page 174 for a more detailed letter template.)

TO _____

THREE WORDS THAT SUM UP HOW I'M FEELING ARE: _____
_____

I WOULD LIKE TO FEEL: _____
_____
_____

WHAT I REALLY NEED TO HELP ME IS: _____
_____

School Stress and Exam Hell

When it comes to school and exams, stress is right up there! There's nothing like the **pressure** of **exam time** to cause some major stress feelings! These guys put it so well:

'I'm under lots of exam pressure and stress at the moment and I don't know how to deal with it. It can get so bad I just have to walk out of whatever class I'm in.'
Sim, 15

'I've just been feeling really stressed lately and I don't know how to control it. Imagine that you are boiling milk and it starts to rise, but you're not allowed to turn the gas off or let the milk flow out of the pan - that's how it feels. It got worse when I changed schools two weeks ago.'
Amelie, 11

'I really care about my grades. Like, REALLY care. I spend hours and hours revising for tests and am always working in some way for something. I guess I do well in school, I get kind of good grades but I can't physically keep working this hard any more. I am constantly tired and have no time to do anything else. Teachers have told me that I over revise and I should cut down a bit because I'm just stressing myself out.'
Olivia, 13

It's important to have what I call a 'healthy dose of perspective' when it comes to school. What I mean by that is, yes, school and your exams are super important, but there is also more to life than just grades and qualifications – they aren't the 'be all and end all'. What's just as important is your health and happiness. There's no point working yourself so hard that you feel ill and can't enjoy any time to relax.

HEADS-UP!

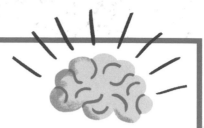

Stress can be a good thing, too! It helps us to focus and to perform better in things like a class presentation or school performance. Once the challenge is over, the stress 'boost' chills and you can recharge your batteries.

What could you do instead of worrying about school? How about channelling some of that stress energy into dancing or sport or reading or crafting or baking ... anything that has your full attention, so you can't think about your feelings.

Hopefully you have nice teachers that you like and who support you. There'll always be that one teacher who you think is a bit of a pain, who pushes you too hard or just doesn't get you. But instead of letting one person wind you up, focus on the people who make you feel good about yourself. It's always a good idea to have a trusted adult in mind to help you offload worries and keep stress to a minimum.

Ask Anna

Dear Anna,

I can't sleep properly at night. I just keep on thinking about things that could happen to me for all different reasons! When I do feel sleepy, I just close my eyes and try to think of happy things, but somehow the bad stuff comes into my head and will not go until I sleep. I would curl up into a ball, my toes would be really wiggling like crazy and they will not stop! What should I do? Do you think I am just stressed out for no reason?

Sam, age 12

Anna says:

Bedtime is the quietest part of the day, when all our worries can surface. If you're struggling to get to sleep, keep a pen and paper by your bed and write down everything on your mind, even the silly stuff. Once it's out of your head, it can feel easier to let it go. Try to ease the stress in your body and toes by lying nice and straight, breathe in and out slowly and deeply. Then, starting from your head and working your way down, gently allow each body part to get heavier and more relaxed. Try playing some relaxing music too, this will help distract any bad thoughts.

 # WHEN STRESS COMES OUT

Stress can find its way out in lots of ways. As well as feeling tearful, having aches and pains, and feeling angry or irritable, there are some more serious signs of intense stress that definitely need understanding and support.

Some of these are:

eating disorders – either eating too much, too little or making yourself sick after eating. People can use food as way to release or control their stress.

self-harm – damaging, injuring or hurting yourself as a way to cope with or express overwhelming feelings of distress.

alcohol and drugs – taking substances to 'numb' the stress or emotional distress.

exercising too much – exercise is a good thing, but not when it's done so much that it starts to have a negative effect (such as feeling overtired, or unhealthy weight loss).

Let's be clear, despite what you may have heard, the majority of people who self-harm (and it's 1 in 10 of all young people at least!) are NOT doing it to show off or attention-seek. They do it to help them cope with overwhelming issues such as bullying, family issues, identity, cultural expectations, a death or abuse. These could all be reasons.

In the worst cases, people who feel this bad can even feel like killing themselves. Now, I know that's a pretty scary thought, but this isn't meant to scare you – remember,

we are learning to be the boss of our mental health.

Awareness is key, so we can make sure we know what to look out for in others, and ourselves, and how to get help if it's needed.

If you or someone you know is showing serious signs of stress, don't stay silent. Talk to a trusted adult and get some help and support immediately.

HEADS-UP!

Let any stress out in a quiet, safe environment: play a sport or go for a walk; listen to a favourite band or song; try holding a stress ball or a squishy; watch a movie that makes you laugh. Laughter is an instant stress buster! Turn off your phone for a bit and maybe stroke or chat to the cat – it's purrrfect as it won't answer back ;-)

MYTH BUSTING

'Self-harm and eating disorders are just girls saying they're stressed and looking for attention.'

BUSTED!

Boys AND girls can self-harm or have an eating disorder as a way of coping with stressful feelings. It is never just attention-seeking behaviour. Girls may cut or scratch parts of their body, but boys might hit or punch themselves or objects to let the feelings out.

Breathe It – Boss It

When we're worried, stressed or anxious, we don't breathe properly – and this can make us feel worse.

You can do this exercise anywhere so it's a good one to have in your mental health toolkit.

Sit somewhere quiet (I find the bathroom is a good place if I can't find anywhere else!) and take in a nice deep breath.

 Place your hands out in front of you on your lap, palms facing up.

 As you take a nice deep breath in through your nose, slowly count with your fingers on one hand ... pause ... then slowly breathe out through your mouth, counting through the five fingers on the other hand.

 The key here is KEEP IT SLOW. Keep focusing on your hands and fingers, and your breathing. Get into a nice, slow rhythm, working your way through your fingers, backwards and forwards, slowing and deepening your breath more each time.

Stress: Sorted.

To Sum It All Up...

Stress is something we all experience at times – the important thing is to make sure you don't let stress fester away inside of you. Talking, laughing and trying new activities is a great way of letting it all out.

Four

- Remind yourself all the time of what makes you a good friend. The best support you can give a friend is to be there to talk and listen.

- Friendships have ups and downs, and can change – and that's okay. Some might not be 'good' for you any more, and sometimes they just fizzle out.

- Find friends who are into the same stuff as you. The more you have in common with someone, the chances are you'll get on really well – making you feel good about yourself.

Out of all the topics in this book, I reckon the trickiest when it comes to keeping our mental and emotional health in tip-top condition is friendship. It's just such a whopper of a big deal! You've probably heard the saying: 'You can't choose your family, but you *can* choose your friends.' Well, it's true, but often more complicated than it sounds.

Friendships are super important in our lives. Often a friendship serves as a place to talk about the stuff you don't want to mention to your family. A friend is someone to share things with in private, and it's often our pals who keep us going when we're having a down day or when stuff gets real. Friendships help us to cope with whatever life throws at us. They should help us feel supported, liked, valued and respected, and should help our confidence and self-esteem grow.

All great news for our mental and emotional health!

But, let's be realistic, **friendships can be tricky** – they can hit a rough patch or take a different direction as you both change. It's at times like these that a heads-up on how to handle certain situations and look after your feelings and behaviour is really helpful.

MAKING FRIENDS

It doesn't matter how old you are, making friends is scary.

What if they don't like me?

What if I say something dumb?

What if they don't think I'm cool?

The first thing to remember is that all the time people around the world are making friends. Look at your parents or siblings and their mates – at some point their friendships started.

Sometimes you meet people at school or at after-school activities – or sometimes on holiday or through other people you know. Making the *right* friends for *you* is what matters. You don't have to have loads either – **just one or two good mates are more than enough!** And I mean *real* friends, not the trillions you might have on social media.

The main thing is that whoever you choose to be friends with – and remember, you *always* have a choice – make sure it's with people who boost your confidence and self-esteem, and who you honestly enjoy hanging out with.

HEADS-UP!

Friends should *never* make you feel bad about yourself. They should never put you down, make you feel unsafe, put you in danger or make fun of things like your sexuality, religion or culture.

That might seem like an obvious thing to say, but friendships, like all relationships, can be a rollercoaster – up and down and all over the place. And in some cases, if you're not enjoying the ride, you might want to get off.

MYTH BUSTING

'Friendships last forever.'

BUSTED!

Some friendships can last a whole lifetime, but others are like seasons – they come and go. If you feel that you aren't getting anything positive from a friend, or you haven't got anything in common any more, then it's perfectly okay (and brave!) to admit that. Some friendships do just drift apart, with no drama, making way for new ones.

HOW TO FIND AND BE A FAB FRIEND

Being a good friend starts with YOU. What's great about you? Are you loyal, chatty, kind, creative, generous, affectionate, supportive? What do you look for in a friend? Often it's the same qualities you have because that's what we value in someone. It's a bit like playing Snap.

When we're feeling good, proud and confident about what makes 'me' great, we give off a feel-good vibe to others. It's like an invisible magnet to people who think, 'Yeah, I'd like a bit of that as a pal!'

TRY THESE SUGGESTIONS TO FIND NEW FRIENDS:

a hobby or club. Look out for someone who likes the same stuff as you – it really helps when you have things in common.

smile and make eye contact. It might sound silly but someone who smiles, and doesn't just look at the floor, looks happy and friendly. It makes everyone feel at ease.

talk to someone new. Perhaps you've noticed a person who could use a pal? If someone is friendly to you, be friendly back.

ask questions. It can be tricky to know what to say sometimes, and you might feel embarrassed or nervous. To get a conversation started and to show you're interested, have a few questions ready like: 'What music are you into?', 'What do you think of Fortnite?' or 'Who are your favourite YouTubers?'

give a compliment, such as 'I love your outfit' or 'I liked what you said in class the other day'. Saying something nice about someone is a really great way to start a friendship.

take your time. If you don't feel up to it, or freeze, don't worry – just try again when you're feeling better.

ANXIETY AND EVERYTHING ELSE

Peer pressure is feeling like you have to do something because your friends are doing it. **Friendships have a huge influence on what we do and think** – whether it's having the same clothes or taste in music. Friends influence our lives so much, which can often be a good thing – perhaps a friend introduces you to a new music artist or hobby. But there might also be times when friends suggest things that aren't so good and that you don't want to join in with. Things like missing school, smoking or being mean to someone. And this can make you feel a little uneasy, alone, worried or even scared.

Social anxiety is when you feel nervous or worried about going to parties or sleepovers, or something where your friends will be – especially if you're unsure about what your friends might get up to and expect you to do, too.

Let's remember that
ANXIETY
is there to PROTECT us.

It doesn't want us to get harmed in any way and it makes you crave the safety of home. Feeling homesick for a place or person is *really* common. It's totally normal but people don't often admit to it for fear of embarrassment or being labelled.

Peer Pressure: Top Tips

It's totally okay to say 'NO'! It is never okay for friends to pressure you into anything. Practise saying 'no' with confidence so that it feels easier when you need to say it.

Avoid uncomfortable or unsafe situations. If you're not physically there, you won't be pressured into anything.

Respect each other. If you say 'no', then you want to be respected for that. So don't judge your friends, either! Respecting each other's choices will keep things chilled. If your friends don't respect you for having the guts to saying 'no', what does it say about them?

Take the lead. Why not suggest doing something else instead, so no one feels awkward?

MY SAFE PLACE

Do you know what's great about the human imagination? It's that no one else can see inside our mind, or experience it. It's something 100 per cent personal and it's something we can use and add to our mental health toolkit to help us feel safe, calm and happy.

Close your eyes and think of somewhere that makes you feel fab. It could be a memory – perhaps on holiday in the sunshine – or maybe you can think of a place you feel relaxed and safe in, such as your cosy couch in front of your favourite TV show. Whenever you feel worried, anxious, stressed or just need to feel safe, close your eyes and imagine yourself in that special place. Take a deep breath and tell yourself you are you, and you're enough.

Social Anxiety: Top Tips

Surround yourself with friends who understand you and make you feel calm and relaxed.

Tell a trusted friend how you are feeling. They can be there for you if things get a bit much.

Keep your breathing calm. Take long, slow, deep breaths to keep anxiety under control.

Tell yourself you're safe. Often we feel anxious about something we think is going to happen, not what actually does happen. Enjoy the moment and try not to think too far ahead.

SOS! Have someone you trust and love on speed-dial so you can call if you need support. Remind yourself, **you are in control!**

BULLIES, BACK OFF!

• •

Bullying is when someone does or says something to upset or hurt another. It can be physical (like hitting or kicking), emotional (like name-calling or threats) or cyber (anything online).

Bullies are often people we don't get along with. But bullying can happen in friendships, too, which can be tricky to deal with. Let's be clear:

bullying is NEVER OKAY. No one has the right to bully you. It is NEVER your fault.

If you're being bullied, **tell someone**. That's the best way to take care of you – mentally and physically.

Just because it could be your mate picking on you, it doesn't make it okay. Talk to a trusted adult or tell another friend how you're feeling. Think about confronting the bully calmly and confidently, to call them out on their behaviour. If it's on social media, block or report anyone saying anything unkind or weird.

Spending so much time online throws up an area of bullying to watch out for. Make sure you stay safe. Check your online friends are actually who they say they are. There are some pretty strange and dodgy adults in this world, who sometimes pretend to be a young person and try and engage in chat and contact with a child or teen under the age of sixteen - this is known as 'grooming' and is a criminal offence. There is a reason for the age restrictions of certain apps and websites - to keep young people as safe as possible. Always share your account passwords with a parent or trusted adult so they can help keep you safe. Never give out any personal details online, such as your address or phone number, or send photos, and never agree to meet up with anyone in person who you've only ever spoken to online.

Let's be honest,

sometimes friends just aren't friendship material any longer. If a friend is constantly leaving you feeling miserable, tired, anxious, stressed ... then this could potentially affect your mental health. These people are 'toxic friends' – friends who are 'all about them', often unsupportive and leave you feeling drained. You have little in common with these people – they only call you when they want something, and they might 'bring you down' or hold you back when it comes to studies or life ambition.

There are a few ways to deal with toxic friends. If you feel there is no going back, it might be best for your mental health to leave the friendship.

WHY IS MY FRIEND BEING SO MEAN? IT'S REALLY STARTING TO UPSET ME.

Ask Anna

Dear Anna,
My friends have been talking about me behind my back and when I try and hang out with them at lunch they ignore me, and start speaking in a different language so I can't join in. My best friend is in a different tutor group so it's hard to find her at lunch sometimes. I don't want to be alone but these other girls make me feel rubbish.
Sita, age 12

Anna says:
Real friends don't treat people like this. Ignoring you and talking about you doesn't sound like friendly behaviour to me. I get that being alone isn't a fun thought, but sometimes being by yourself is better than putting up with rubbish friends. How about you arrange to meet your best friend at a certain place at lunchtime, and perhaps see who else

is around who might make another good friend? Maybe there's someone who often seems to be by themselves who you could go and say 'hi' to. If friends don't make you feel welcome, don't bother getting into an argument, just walk away and hold your head up high. Find someone who deserves your friendship.

How to Leave a Friendship

BE HONEST

Look for pals who are into the same things as you, and make you feel energized and happy. A good test is to gauge how you feel when they message or call you. If you feel pleased, they're a good friend to have. If you feel dread when your phones pings, they're not the mate for you.

DON'T BE TOO AVAILABLE

Make sure you don't pounce on messages the minute they hit your inbox, and don't be too quick to hear the latest story that is likely to make you feel rubbish. Create some distance so your friend realizes you're not at their beck and call.

 ## SAY HOW YOU FEEL

Tell them how they've been making you feel and give them a chance to explain. You never know, it might just be the wake-up call they need to turn things around. If not, you deserve some new friends!

 ## MAKE SOME NEW FRIENDS

As easy as it sounds. Go get 'em kid!

Friendships: Sorted. Well done!

To Sum It All Up...

Friendships are super important, but always remember what makes you a great pal, and that YOU get to choose who to be friends with.

Five

- New feelings, thoughts and urges might feel weird and confusing – talk to a pal, adult or sibling to reassure yourself about what's going on.

- Everyone develops, physically and mentally, at different rates – everyone is in the same boat, eventually.

- You are in control at all times! Never feel pressured into doing anything you don't feel ready for or comfortable doing.

SEX!

There you go, I've said it. Ha ha, yep – we've hit the chapter that you might think is the embarrassing and awkward stuff. Shall we just get the snigger-inducing words we're going to be using out there now?

WILLY, penis, breasts, vagina, PERIOD, sex, puberty, BRA, kissing, SANITARY TOWELS!

There, now we can all stop cringing. But, here's the thing – talking about our bodies, thoughts and feelings shouldn't be awkward or embarrassing. After all, **we're only human**! We all use the loo (even the Queen!), we all have private parts and we all get a bit confused or weirded out from time to time when stuff happens.

It doesn't matter how well clued up or not you are about puberty, it can still be a pretty big deal when it happens, and a lot to get your head round. The official definition of 'puberty' is:

Puberty
noun

'When an adolescent reaches sexual maturity and is capable of reproduction.'

Wow, that's a pretty big statement. What does it even mean?! Let's break it down, as understanding physical changes can really help you get to grips with emotional changes.

Basically, when we reach a certain age, our bodies change, allowing us to have sex and children, should we want to. It might sound scary and a lot to take in, but it really is nothing to be worried or concerned about. In fact, it's a really exciting development – it's **perfectly normal and natural**! But, it's important to remember that everyone develops at different times.

WHAT'S GOING ON?

On average, girls hit puberty a bit earlier than boys, between eight and thirteen years old. Boys tend to start puberty between the ages of ten and sixteen. During this time, girls can expect to see physical changes, such as:

- their breasts growing
- periods starting
- hair growing in some pretty interesting places (armpits, legs, around the vagina)

Boys will experience changes of their own, such as:

- hair growth on their face, body and willy,
- their penis growing,
- their voice getting deeper

Change can be **SCARY** and **OVERWHELMING**. But remember – if we learn about why something is happening, we're looking after our mental and emotional health as well as understanding the physical changes. So, fear not – if it seems like you're the only girl in the PE changing room wearing a bra or using sanitary towels, or if you're the only guy who hasn't got muscles and hair 'down there' yet – trust me, you're not alone! Our bodies develop at different rates and whether you're the first or last to grow boobs or get a deep voice, once everyone has caught up it won't even be a big deal any more.

MYTH BUSTING

'Girls are more mature than boys.'

BUSTED!
Girls tend to start puberty a year or two earlier than boys. But girls are not more mature than boys, they just get a bit of a head start in the growing-up process.

WHAT ARE THESE NEW FEELINGS?

As you notice your **body changing**, you may experience new and **unfamiliar** feelings or urges. These are usually brought about by 'hormonal' changes. You may have heard an adult talk about you, or someone else, being a moody teenager, or that so-and-so is full of raging hormones. Well, hormones are essentially signals from your brain to your baby-making bits. The hormones ramp up feelings of sexual arousal – when we feel excited and our private parts feel good to touch, and we might consider doing something for pleasure with them one day.

This is the time when we might start to fancy people –

CLASSMATES. *friends*, celebrities OFF THE *telly*...

The thought of kissing and touching them (and vice versa!) and spending time with them suddenly feels rather appealing. As your friends start to experience similar thoughts and feelings, the focus starts to shift to forming intense, romantic and sometimes sexual relationships.

You might see that some people in your year, whose bodies have perhaps developed more quickly than others, are suddenly getting loads of attention. It can be a really **stressful** time trying to keep up, especially if you're not quite as grown-up yet. But never feel the need to rush it – your body is your body, and no matter how annoying it can be, it will **develop** in its own time.

HEADS-UP!

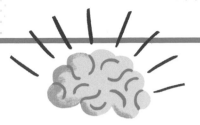

Parents can get really aggy about teens 'staying up too late' or 'lolling around in bed'. However, here's something to show that you're not just lazy! During puberty there is a natural internal shift that causes teenagers to feel more alert later at night. The problem is, you still have to get up early for school, so this is often why teens get stick for being moody and wanting to sleep in at the weekends.

UH OHH...

EVEN *more*
awkwardness!

Do you sometimes have days when you doubt yourself? When you think:

'Who am I and what do I want from life'?

And your head feels a bit full? If so, then welcome to the club. As we grow up and experience different things it's perfectly normal to lose track of what we like and where we're heading. Sometimes it can all be rather confusing.

Your teenage years are a time of **change** and **experimentation** – some things you think about and try doing now might just stay in the past ... and for some things that's probably not so bad, LOL.

Expressing feelings, experiencing attractions and **developing sexuality** is a healthy and natural phase that everyone goes through (yep, even your parents went through it – yuck!). Finding ways to connect with people you like is an exciting but nerve-wracking time. You may start by just chatting at school during lunch, or outside of school at sports clubs or online ... anywhere!

Getting to know someone and finding out more about them is a great way of working out how much you like them, and indeed if you **LIKE** like them enough to want to 'go out' with them. Kissing and flirting can lead to more urges and a desire to be more physically active, such as taking part in sexual acts. It's a **LOT** to think about so it's always super important never to rush into any of these decisions. Talk it over with friends and people you trust to make sure you're taking care of not only your physical self, but also that boiling pot of emotions and feelings in your head.

HEADS-UP!

In the UK, the law says you have be over sixteen to consent to have sex – whatever your sexuality. The law is not there to jail under-sixteens who might choose to have sex with each other (although it is still illegal!). The law is there to protect young people from exploitation or abuse.

IDENTIT(Y)

Sometimes, it can be hard to really know who we are. Mates, social media, things we may have already experienced can all hugely influence who we become, what we like and who we like. As the teen years sneak in, someone hot may catch your eye and you end up thinking,

'Hmm, I wouldn't mind getting to know YOU!'

Now, this might be someone of the opposite sex or you, might fancy someone who is the same sex as you or even both sexes! Whether you're gay, straight or bisexual,

experimenting with your feelings and sexuality is a really important and normal part of **developing** your **identity**. It doesn't necessarily mean you will identify in the same way later in life. It's okay to change your mind.

Alongside working out who you fancy, puberty is also a time where worry may start brewing over sexual or gender identity. You might have heard about people being **gender-fluid, gender-neutral** or **transgender**. This means that the individual perhaps doesn't wish to be, or believe they are, the gender they were born as.

MYTH BUSTING

'You're gay if you fancy someone the same sex as you.'

BUSTED!
Actually, no. Experimenting is part of exploring who you are. Fancying someone of the same gender doesn't automatically mean you identify one way or another.

For example, a girl might decide she doesn't want to be a girl, and instead would like to be a boy, and vice versa

– a boy may decide he'd prefer to be girl. Experimenting with clothing choices, make-up and hairstyles, and taking part in activities the opposite sex would perhaps more typically do, are all positive ways to try things out.

Sadly, you might not always be met with positive comments and opinions, but that says more about anyone making the rubbish comments than it does about you.

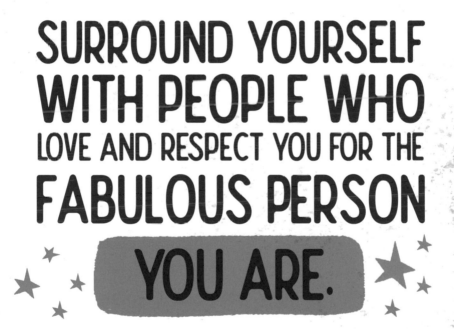

SURROUND YOURSELF WITH PEOPLE WHO LOVE AND RESPECT YOU FOR THE FABULOUS PERSON YOU ARE.

Take everything at your own pace – the ultimate goal is to find comfort, acceptance and self-confidence in celebrating yourself.

CRACKING ON
AND CALLING iT A
DAY

Relationships are a huge part of life. Some will be amazing to remember and some we'd rather leave behind us. It's all part of exploring who you enjoy spending time with and who, ultimately, makes you feel good. A healthy relationship should make you feel safe, happy, in control and confident. A great relationship, which should involve trust and respect, can in time turn into the ultimate status change – **marriage.**

The best chance of finding a person you get on with is seeking out someone who has similar likes and interests to you. Maybe you have similar families, or live on the same road. Perhaps you are in the same class, go to the same after-school club or have the same taste in music. Telling someone you like them is perhaps the hardest and most awkward thing to do.

ALWAYS
REMIND YOURSELF OF WHAT'S
GREAT
ABOUT YOU!

If you like yourself, someone else is going to too.

There are times when relationships don't work out. No matter how amazing and 'totes in love' you might have once felt, the reality is that a lot of relationships can change and end (we've all seen *Love Island*, right?!). That's okay, it's part of life and even though it can suck

big time and hurt in a lot of cases, just remember that any initial upset you feel **WILL** ease off over time. If someone is being mean to you, making you feel bad about yourself, pressuring you into something you're not comfortable with, or if you're just feeling a bit unsure – do speak to someone you trust, preferably an adult. Explain calmly yet firmly what you will and won't put up with. If someone makes you feel rubbish, then they're not the one for you.

GETTING TO KNOW SOMEONE

Okay, so you like someone. Your head is full of thoughts of them ... you wonder what they're doing all day ... you think about what it might be like to get to know them better. Here are some tips to boost your confidence:

body language. How you carry yourself says a lot. Someone shy might have hunched shoulders, feet scuffing on the floor, a scruffy appearance... Flip this on its head, literally! Hold your head up, make eye contact, plaster a big smile on your face – you'll instantly appear more friendly and attractive.

think of some 'open questions' you could ask to get conversation going (these are questions that require more than just a 'yes' or 'no' answer). Some great examples are: 'What is your favourite type of music?'; 'What are you up to this weekend?'; 'Where's the best place you've ever been?' Hopefully they will say some of the same things you like. This is a great way to get to know someone.

feeling nervous is perfectly normal. In fact, nerves show that you're human and that you care. Don't worry if you appear nervous talking to the person you like – just remind yourself of what a great catch you are, take a nice deep breath and go for it.

Ask Anna

Dear Anna,
There's this guy that I really like and he told me he likes me too, but if I do go out with him I know he'll just want sex and I don't think I'm ready. But everyone else seems to be losing their virginity, so maybe I should too?
Chanel, age 14

Anna says:

It might seem like everyone is losing their virginity, but the chances are they aren't! They are most likely feeling exactly like you are – not ready – and that is totally okay. In fact, it's more than okay!

It's so important that you never rush into anything and that you think properly about what you might want to do, when, and who with. Anyone that pressures you into having sex, or doing anything you're not comfortable with, doesn't deserve to be intimate with you. Be strong and confident in telling someone to wait. **NEVER** feel you have to do something just because others are doing it.

YOU'RE THE **BOSS**

A really popular way to meet people is online and on apps. But you might bump into people you like and want to get to know IRL, too. However you meet, it's important to be clear about what you would like from the relationship. Talking and communicating with the person you've decided to share your private time with is key to making sure you are in control and feel comfortable at all times.

Chatting it over with your mates is important, as they will always have an opinion and some good advice. Their seal of approval is usually a big deal! If you're not ready to do anything intimate, even kissing, then that's totally cool. Giving 'consent' is when you give permission to take part in something intimate – you have the right to say 'no' at any time, even if you previously said 'yes' and then changed your mind. **The person you are with must respect your decision.**

Think carefully about whether you feel ready to share yourself with someone. Make sure you have thought about any necessary safety precautions, like birth control. Have a think about how you might feel afterwards to ensure you're making a good decision. Being intimate should be fun, should make you feel good, and be something enjoyed by both of you.

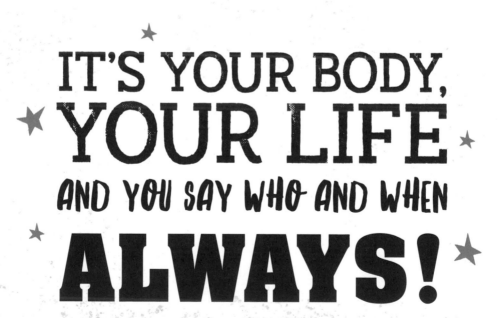

IT'S YOUR BODY,
YOUR LIFE
AND YOU SAY WHO AND WHEN
ALWAYS!

STAY SAFE

Something else you might come across is 'sexting' – this is sharing explicit, or 'sexy', images by text or social media. Once a photo has been sent we lose complete control over where it has gone – and where it might go in the future! **It gets launched into cyberspace forever.**

If someone asks you to send a picture of yourself naked, ask yourself – would a caring, nice person be asking for this? Even if they say it's just for them, you can never be sure it will stay that way. Imagine if it got into the hands of the wrong people! A hacker, people from school, your teachers, or even worse – your parents!

If you're not sure what's okay, a good rule is to not send anything to anyone that you wouldn't want your granny to see. That way you can be completely in control. I mentioned 'grooming' in the last chapter, and it's important in this chapter too.

REMEMBER TO BE SMART!

Be aware of who you are chatting to online. Are they who they say they are? Never send photos or give out any private information like your address or school details. Always tell a trusted adult if an online friend has asked to meet you face-to-face.

Childline has loads of safety tips on how to stay safe online and dating IRL, as well as guidance on reporting and blocking anyone you're uncomfortable with on social media.

Dating: Sorted.

To Sum It All Up...

We're all learning about ourselves all the time. Exploring, embracing and accepting who you are will help you be the boss of your emotional and mental health.

Love and Loss

- Families have ups and downs. Arguments are perfectly normal, but your family should be a secure and safe place.

- Being upset when you've lost someone – grieving – is normal. Don't hide or keep your feelings in, let them out to someone you trust.

- Surround yourself with all the things in your life that make you feel good.

Let's be honest – **families can sometimes be a complete pain in the butt!** We already know that parents can stress us out when it comes to school, exams and stuff in general. In this chapter we're going to look at how else parents and families may cause worry and upset – stuff that can impact our mental health if we don't look after ourselves.

You may have heard this saying:

YOU CAN CHOOSE YOUR FRIENDS, BUT YOU CAN'T CHOOSE YOUR FAMILY

It's pretty true, huh? Something else that's true is that there is no such thing as the perfect family. Social media, magazines and movies can sometimes make us feel as though everyone else has it sooooo good, but the reality is that for most of us, families can cause drama – and not all of it's fun!

Families can face all kinds of issues, such as divorce and separation, moving house, arguments, physical or mental abuse, not looking after each other properly, drug or alcohol problems, health problems, domestic violence, money worries, cultural differences – the list goes on and on! Occasional arguments and bickering is totally normal, and often quite helpful at sorting out an issue, but overall, **home should be a safe place where you feel loved.**

Families should be happy (most of the time!), safe and secure. Of course, we all have rubbish days when we want to yell and slam a door – that's a sign that stress has bubbled over. But when everything has calmed down, we have a right to feel happy and relaxed. **If you're feeling stressed, anxious or sad, don't hold it in.** Definitely talk to an adult you trust to get some help. If you ever feel in danger, call 999 or speak to a doctor, counsellor or teacher – to let them know how you're feeling about family stuff.

WHEN PARENTS
Break UP!

Maybe your parents are still together, or
perhaps you have a step-parent or your mum
or dad is a single parent, and it's always been like that...
However your family is made up, it's completely unique –
there is no right or wrong way to be a family! What is
right though is that you're allowed to feel exactly as you
wish, especially if things happen that you're not over the
moon about.

If two parents have brought you up, chances are you want
them to stay together. There are, of course, some times
when you might feel it would be better for everyone if
they were apart, but usually having your parents together
is what you want. Sadly, it doesn't always work out like

this, and in some cases, parents choose to not be with each other any more and split up.

If this happens, it can be a time of worry and change. **What will happen? Where we all live? When will I see my mum/dad?** Feeling not in control of any of these things is really upsetting.

Parents might break up for loads of different reasons, and whatever the reason, it's a very personal time and they might not want to tell you why. But if it's bugging you and you feel it's important that you know, your parents owe you an explanation. You should feel as included and respected as possible.

A break-up affects the whole family, not just your parents.

If something like this happens to your family, you will probably have lots of questions and thoughts racing through your head. **The unknown can be really scary.**

Not many people like change when it's forced on them! It's important that you take care of yourself and for you to understand that **if you're feeling bad in any way, it's okay.**

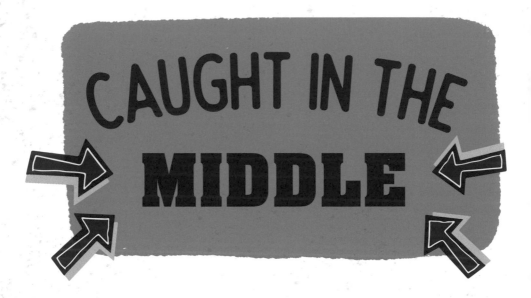

If you parents split up, you might need to move home or school, or be told when you can and can't see the other parent. You might be asked to make choices, too – such as who to live with – that might make you feel confused and guilty. This is all a LOT to take on so always make sure you talk to your parents, either separately or together, to tell them how it's all making you feel so they can help you adjust to any changes. If you can't talk to your parents, talk to another adult you trust.

CALLUM HAS BEEN FEELING CAUGHT IN THE MIDDLE:

'My mum and dad divorced when I was four. I'm now fourteen. I stopped talking to my dad when I was seven as my mum used to tell me horrible stuff about him, but now I've grown up I realize that it's just because she's angry at him, and doesn't want me to get upset by him. I want to have a bond with him but the last time I approached him I had a huge argument with my mum about it. I really want to talk to him again, but I'm worried about asking her...'

AND INDI IS FEELING THE HEAT FROM HER MUM AND DAD, TOO :

'My mum and dad are constantly arguing and they are dragging me into it. I'm getting really worried - they have said they're getting divorced, but I don't really understand any of it.'

Neither Callum or Indi deserve the stress and sadness that their parents breaking up has caused them. **Always talk to your parents to let them know how you feel.** A break-up is very emotional for everyone in the family, and even though it may seem like it's their fault, parents can get so caught up in their own feelings and in juggling the situation that they might forget how much it's affecting you.

Choose a good time to speak to your mum or dad, or both, when they're not busy (maybe on the way home from school or during evening downtime), or you might find it easier to write your thoughts and feelings down in a letter and give it to them to read – this can help when you feel a bit stuck for what to say. See page 174 for a letter template, to help you decide what to write.

REMEMBER:

iF YOUR PARENTS BREAK UP, iT iS NOT YOUR FAULT!

MORE THE MERRIER OR
DOUBLE
TROUBLE

If parents divorce, they might then go on to meet someone else they want to be with. Perhaps this person has kids of their own, and you might find yourself feeling confused, **overwhelmed** or unsure about how things are going to be with these new people in your life. You also might not want to share your mum or dad with someone new! That's totally fair enough. After all, you didn't ask for these changes to happen. But, don't worry – we're going to boss any weird feelings. **Remember, you're in charge of how you feel,** and you shouldn't pretend to feel a certain way to keep other people happy – it'll just make you feel worse.

Change can be scary. But in time, it can be a positive thing, too. And if the general vibe in your family life is happier, then that's definitely something good to hang on to. Having a 'second family' is becoming more and more

common. Chances are you know quite a few people your age who have a step-parent and step- or half-siblings.

HEADS-UP!

A stepfamily, sometimes called a 'blended family', is when two families come together. Sometimes they decide to live together in the same house to create a new, 'second' family.

A new family set-up can be pretty emotional, and everyone needs time to get used to it. Never feel as though you have to suddenly be okay with everything straightaway. There might be different or unfamiliar ways of doing things, new rules to get used to and different personalities to get to know.

You might really like your new step-parent or siblings, or they might not be your cup of tea just yet – or ever. You might not like sharing your mum or dad with this new person and their kids, or perhaps you feel torn and guilty towards your other parent for actually getting on with your new stepmum or stepdad. **It's totally okay to feel all these things.** It's also okay to prefer your own parent over your step-parent, and to not love the situation as much as they want you to.

Spending time together, planning activities or days out, and talking openly and honestly about your feelings will help your stepfamily to get to know each other. **Don't bottle up any thoughts and feelings.**

With good communication and plenty of time, there is every chance that your second family will become a really positive place for you. But if at any time you're not feeling it, **DO talk to a trusted adult for support.**

How to Talk to Parents – SO THEY ACTUALLY LISTEN

Knowing what to say when, and how to say it, can be tricky! Here are some tips to help you find your voice when you need to be heard:

Write it down: you don't need to write a script, but some points to help you remember what you want to talk about will give you some confidence to start with.

 Choose your time and place: have a think about when is the best time to talk. Make sure it's when your parents are chilled and have time to listen properly – not when they're stressed from work, making dinner and juggling a million things. (There's a letter template on page 174.)

 Be honest: tell them exactly how you're feeling – the more they know, the more they can do to support you and help you get it off your chest.

 Don't argue: you will be taken much more seriously and the chat will go better if you can stay as positive and mature as possible.

 Listen: a talk will be so much better if you listen back to the person you're talking to. Both of you will feel respected and it can help you to reach a good decision.

MYTH BUSTING

'Stepfamilies or blended families are on the increase.'

BUSTED!

This is true. Blended or stepfamilies (which usually is made up of at least one step-parent, step-siblings, and/or half-siblings and single parents) are gradually replacing the birth family, where you live with both your mum and dad.

Losing Someone You Love

Lots of people are worried about or scared by the thought of someone they love leaving or dying. You may have already experienced loss, or bereavement, and the feelings that happen afterwards. **It can be a traumatic and upsetting time.** No one knows how they might feel if someone or something they are used to goes away. And it's not just death that can make us feel bad – we can be just as upset if someone we love moves away, or if a sibling leaves home, a family pet dies or if someone gets ill and changes.

There is no 'one way' to cope or deal with losing someone. Everyone experiences different feelings, at different times. You might feel confused, like you can't handle things, or you might feel scared, numb, out of control or angry. **You might feel all of these things.** Accepting how you feel is really important, and often having a good cry is a great way of letting some of those feelings out. **Boys and men absolutely cry too! Crying is a healthy sign of strength and bravery.**

If someone you know has died suddenly or you've seen something on the news that has upset you, or you might have witnessed something terrible, then you can experience feelings of shock, intense sadness and depression. Sometimes this is called post-traumatic stress disorder (PTSD). It's nothing to be scared of, but it's important that a doctor, counsellor or medical professional helps you through the feelings it can cause.

HEADS-UP!

Worrying about a parent dying or getting ill is really common and can cause anxious feelings. Sometimes we worry too much about our own health, too, and that can stop us doing day-to-day things. This is called 'health anxiety'. Make sure you talk to someone you trust so they can help reassure you and reduce any anxious feelings.

Do you worry about people not telling you the truth and keeping things from you? Adults often do this to try and protect you, but it can sometimes backfire and make you feel more anxious. Just let them know that it would make you feel more trusting and less anxious if you ALWAYS knew the truth.

Ask Anna

Dear Anna,

My mum died nearly two months ago and I'm having trouble sleeping and coping at school. Plus my boyfriend broke up with me shortly afterwards. I have extreme mood swings and anxiety and really miss my mum.

Jo, age 15

Anna says:

Oh Jo, sending a massive hug. You've had a lot of emotional upheaval to cope with recently, so it's no wonder your mood is up and down. Your anxious feelings are a response from the upset you have gone through. Anxiety is your body's way of letting out stressful, upsetting feelings.

It's natural to miss your mum. And there are ways you can keep her memory precious. In time, the pain will hopefully be a little more manageable. See if you have a school counsellor you can speak to, to help you work through your feelings. Are there any family members you can talk to for support? You might not feel like it, but hobbies and activities, such as the gym or a sport, can help distract you from the intense feelings of loss – exercise is proven to help lift mood and ease anxiety. It might be that some short-term medication to help is something to chat over with your family and doctor, too.

MYTH BUSTING

'Time heals.'

BUSTED!

It can be really annoying when people say 'time heals'. When you're hurting inside it can feel as though the horrible feelings won't ever go away. But time can help to lessen the pain and upset of missing someone or something. Time doesn't take the feeling away but it can make the feeling easier to cope with and help you remember what you're missing in a less upsetting way.

HOW TO REMEMBER *someone*

Losing someone can be super tough, but it can be really comforting to remember special times. Here's a few ways to enjoy thinking good things about the person you've lost:

 Talk about them: tell funny stories, remember all the good things and enjoy sharing what you loved and miss about them. There's a great saying: 'gone, but not forgotten.'

 Talk to them: it might sound a bit bonkers, but imagine them and tell them everything that's going on in your life and how you're feeling. You may even like to write them a letter to say all the things you'd tell them if they were here.

Go to a special place: perhaps you have somewhere you enjoyed going to together, or maybe they have a resting place, such as a grave, that you can visit to feel close.

 Mark the occasion: do something special on a certain day that feels important – maybe the day the loved one went away or their birthday.

 **Make a memory box:** decorate and fill a box with some of their things, perhaps photos or some belongings that remind you of them. Whenever you feel sad, bring the box out and look at all the things for comfort.

Loss Sorted. Well done!

To Sum It All Up...

Sometimes things happen in life that we can't control or change. It's important to talk about your feelings to help you feel better and look to the future.

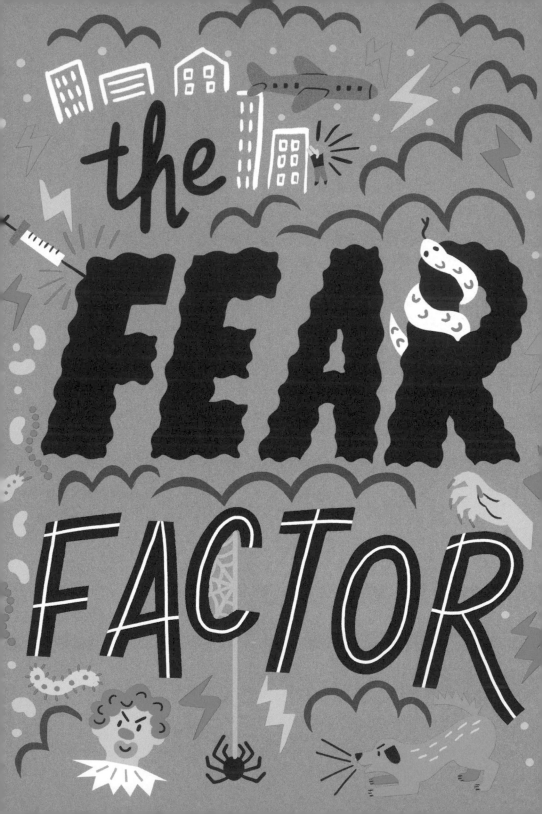

Seven

• Phobias are part of the anxiety family. Understanding what the feelings are and why we react to certain things will help you boss them.

• Face your phobia! It's the best way to kick it to the curb. Sounds pretty terrifying, but it really can help.

• Slow and steady all the way. Be kind to yourself! Take confronting your fears one step at a time – rushing it can freak you out even more.

A phobia is an intense, often irrational, fear of something. The reactions and feelings linked to phobias are similar to what we looked at in the anxiety and panic attack chapter. But the difference with a phobia is that it makes you avoid the thing that causes the intense fear.

You might know about phobias already. Loads of people have phobias about all kinds of things and cope just fine day-to-day. It's when people are faced with the thing they fear, or go out of their way to avoid it, that the phobia becomes a bigger issue. Snakes, spiders, heights, speaking in public... There are hundreds of phobias. But where do they come from? And why do we develop them? A phobia, like anxiety, is something deep-rooted in our mind and body that tries to protect us when **danger comes a-knocking**. But here's the thing – we can actually learn to be fearful. Sounds a bit odd, doesn't it? **Who on earth would want to learn to be scared?** But our brains are pretty nifty and often do their own thing. Your brain stores up memories and thoughts, which can plant the seed of a phobia.

SOWING THE SEED

Some fears are really normal and natural, and start from an early age – such as a fear of being left alone. But these early fears usually come and go quickly. As we get older, bigger phobias can spring up. Some really common fears are of:

- **INJECTIONS**
- **THE DARK**
- **SPEAKING IN FRONT OF PEOPLE**
- **PARENTS SPLITTING UP**

Perhaps you could add to the list:

_____

_____

Phobias develop for different reasons. You might see or experience something upsetting and decide to avoid doing it again. Or perhaps you might pick up phobias that other people have. Sometimes people tell us something should be feared (such as spiders or injections) and so we create a belief that we must never get involved with that thing. This is called **learned behaviour** and it's pretty much how all big phobias start.

IN SHORT, PHOBIAS ARE FEARS WE PICK UP ON THAT DEVELOP AND TAKE HOLD, AND BOOM - GET TRIGGERED EVERY TIME WE THINK OF, OR ARE CONFRONTED WITH, THE SCARY THING.

ITTY-BITTY
TO
NITTY-GRITTY

If we experience something we don't like, and don't do anything about it, it can turn from an itty-bitty niggle into a gigantic issue.

This book is all about being honest, so I'm going to share two phobias of mine to help you make some sense of how these extreme fears can set in.

When I was thirteen, my dad was really ill. The sight of him in hospital, all hooked up to machines and talking absolute nonsense due to his medicine, scared me – I was terrified he was going to die. Thankfully, he got better, but ever since then I've carried around a fear of him getting poorly. I then lost my beloved nanny and uncle really close together, so it felt like everyone I cared about was leaving, and it was a very scary and unpredictable feeling. My phobia of death (called 'thanatophobia') had well and truly begun. I would do everything I could to avoid hospitals and talking about my family's well-being.

Now, every time my dad goes to see his doctor, I get a totally irrational whoosh of fear and panic and instantly think he is dying. He's not, but it doesn't stop the intense feeling of anxiety whenever I hear about a family member being ill.

Since I was about eight, I've also had one of the most common phobias – fear of spiders! I shriek and run a mile if I see a little eight-legged creature scuttle by. It can actually be rather embarrassing – I once jumped so far in fear that I threw my drink over someone!

And that's the thing – we can't help how we physically and emotionally react to sudden, intense fear.

SPIDE—EURGHS

My spider phobia started how it does for most people – by learning from various sources that spiders pose a threat and should be feared. Movies and TV shows don't help – there are loads of things that make spiders out to be scary (like *I'm a Celebrity, Get Me Out of Here!* or Aragog from Harry Potter). But if I think about it, what have spiders done to me? Have they hurt me or attacked me? Nope. I don't like the way they look, but that's not exactly their fault, is it?

My spider phobia was learned from my nanny. As a kid I picked up on her behaviour – when she saw a spider she would freak out until someone removed it. I adored my nanny – she protected me, so I believed and copied everything she did and said. She (unwisely!) told me a story about a tarantula (I won't share it, I don't want to pass on any fear to you!), which is where she got her phobia. And there you have it – a phobia passed on from generation to generation, even when **nothing bad had ever actually happened.**

WHEN FEAR turns to PHOBIA

SHHHH!

MWAHAHAHAHA

20 YEARS LATER...

OVER THE YEARS I HAVE DISCOVERED A LOT OF TECHNIQUES TO HELP CALM MY IRRATIONAL FEARS. UNDERSTANDING AND WORKING THROUGH FEARS AND PHOBIAS, AND THINKING ABOUT THEM IN A DIFFERENT WAY, CAN MASSIVELY HELP.

TOP TERRORS

There are **SO MANY** phobias. Fear of germs, heights, injections, being sick, blood, thunderstorms, clowns, balloons, trees, feet...

It's important never to laugh at or make fun of anyone who is experiencing a phobia – even if their fear or reaction seems odd. There will always be a reason why that fear is there, and understanding and supporting someone with a phobia really can help them. **Here are some really common phobias:**

Aerophobia – fear of flying. This might not cause a problem day-to-day but could be tricky when it comes to family holidays or school trips abroad.

Cynophobia – a fear of dogs. This one can take hold if someone has been bitten or frightened by a dog.

Arachnophobia – fear of spiders. This can be a learned behaviour or perhaps develop after an upsetting personal experience.

Ophidiophobia – fear of snakes. Movies are full of 'scary' snakes, or maybe someone once tried to scare you with a fake snake? This can also be a learned behaviour.

Social phobia – fear of going out with or being around people. This can affect school attendance and enjoyment, speaking in front of people or going to parties.

Agoraphobia – fear of crowds or of being in a public place where you feel helpless or unable to escape easily. This can lead to fearing certain places or modes of transport if the initial panic or anxiety creates a lasting memory.

Claustrophobia – fear of being in small spaces. This can happen in places such as lifts, aeroplanes or tube trains.

Nomophobia – fear of being without your phone. This is a big step up from just being upset if you've forgotten your phone – genuine panic and anxiety sets in.

MYTH BUSTING

'We're born with only two phobias.'

BUSTED!
Correct! The only two fears we are born with are a fear of loud noises and the fear of falling. Everything else is learned.

How Does a PHOBIA FEEL?

Someone who is scared of flying might manage their phobia pretty well day-to-day and avoid going on planes. However, unless they confront it eventually, this won't help them in the long run – the minute they have to fly somewhere then that pesky phobia will rear its ugly head.

Phobias like social anxiety can be trickier to live with. A fear of being around classmates, teachers, crowds, and a fear of speaking in class, can all prove really stressful to manage and live with. Some people worry about needing the loo at school, or being sick in class, or saying something dumb and being laughed at – social anxieties like these can be really tough to deal with.

A phobia can fill you with shame and embarrassment. The uncontrollable reaction that happens (such as me jumping and spilling drinks over people!) keeps the feeling of shame hidden.

Having a phobia does <u>NOT</u> mean you are weak.

It can feel like everyone is looking at you – they're not, but your mind can play tricks on you when you're feeling anxious.

- FEEL SHAKY
- GET SWEATY
- HAVE HOT FLUSHES OR CHILLS
- FEEL BREATHLESS
- HAVE A RACING HEART
- GET BUTTERFLIES IN YOUR TUMMY
- FEEL SICK
- BECOME PANICKY
- NEED THE LOO
- FEELING LIKE YOU'RE GOING TO FAINT.

Remember that the same phobia can affect people differently. Just because one person who doesn't like snakes only has a tiny fear response, it doesn't mean that someone else who screams and cries is in any way over-reacting. They are both responding to the same fear response, just on different levels. And saying that someone who has a strong reaction is 'being silly' will just make the phobia worse.

HEADS-UP!

Like we've just said, there are lots of natural reactions to phobias. **You might cry, shiver, run away, scream or leg it to the loo**... Your reaction is your mind hitting your 'anxiety panic button' and trying to keep you safe. Even when the situation is not threatening, you can lose all sense of reality if your mind screams 'danger'. The response is every bit as real as if it were an actual threat. You often know your reaction doesn't make sense – it's 'irrational' – but you just can't help it.

BACK TO BASICS!

We often don't remember when and how a phobia first began. It can be helpful to think back and work out when the fear took hold, and then ask yourself questions about how you could have felt and reacted differently.

If you can't recall why the phobia kicked in, try to change your panicky thoughts into sensible questions and statements. Let's use my spider phobia as an example:

what has a spider ever done to me?

can it help looking the way it does? How would I feel if someone screamed at me for the way I looked and moved?

spiders are great at getting rid of annoying insects, like flies.

I'm hundreds of times bigger than a spider, so who should be more scared of who? No wonder they run away so fast when they see me coming!

a spider has never actually hurt me.

Turning my fears upside down and into positive thoughts chills out my fear factor and anxiety – **it completely calms me down.**

Ask Anna

Dear Anna,

I'm having a really difficult time at school. I think I might have a school phobia. I'm in the middle of my GCSEs but I'm missing lots of my lessons due to the fear of being around people in class. I have panic attacks when I try to go in. I know younger children can have a school phobia, but is it possible for me to as well?

Robbie, age 15

Anna says:

Anyone can develop a phobia, and it sounds like school is really stressful for you at the moment. Perhaps a panic attack at school started your worry about going in, and the thought of having another attack made you worry more? That's exactly how a phobia can start.

Speak to your parents and teachers to explain how you're feeling – ask them for help and support. Speak to your school counsellor or doctor, too, for extra help with your anxiety and panic attacks. Working through how and why the phobia started, and facing it one step at a time, will help it to go away.

THE **FEAR** LADDER!

The best way to conquer a phobia is to face it. Sounds pretty **eek**, but trust me – it's the avoidance of a fear that makes it get worse. **Be the super brave person I know you are** – create your own Fear Ladder!

A Fear Ladder breaks your phobia down into manageable steps. At the top of your ladder is your phobia and each rung of the ladder is a step closer to beating it. The aim is to climb up, rung by rung, gradually busting your fears.

Choose between eight and ten doable steps that climb up to your phobia and rate each one for how fearful of it you feel – 1 for the lowest and 10 for the highest.

The aim is to keep repeating each step, checking how anxious you feel, until you no longer feel any fear.

Only when the fear has completely gone should you move up a rung. Tell a parent or friend what you're doing so you have their support. **Don't rush it!**

Here's an example Fear Ladder, using my spider phobia, to give you an idea of how it works.

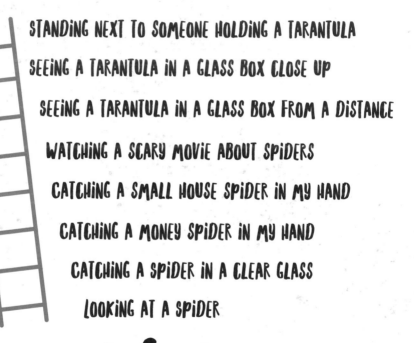

STANDING NEXT TO SOMEONE HOLDING A TARANTULA

SEEING A TARANTULA IN A GLASS BOX CLOSE UP

SEEING A TARANTULA IN A GLASS BOX FROM A DISTANCE

WATCHING A SCARY MOVIE ABOUT SPIDERS

CATCHING A SMALL HOUSE SPIDER IN MY HAND

CATCHING A MONEY SPIDER IN MY HAND

CATCHING A SPIDER IN A CLEAR GLASS

LOOKING AT A SPIDER

Phobias: Sorted.

To Sum It All Up...

Remember, anyone and everyone has fears. We are all unique and having a fear is nothing to be ashamed of or embarrassed about – in fact it's normal!

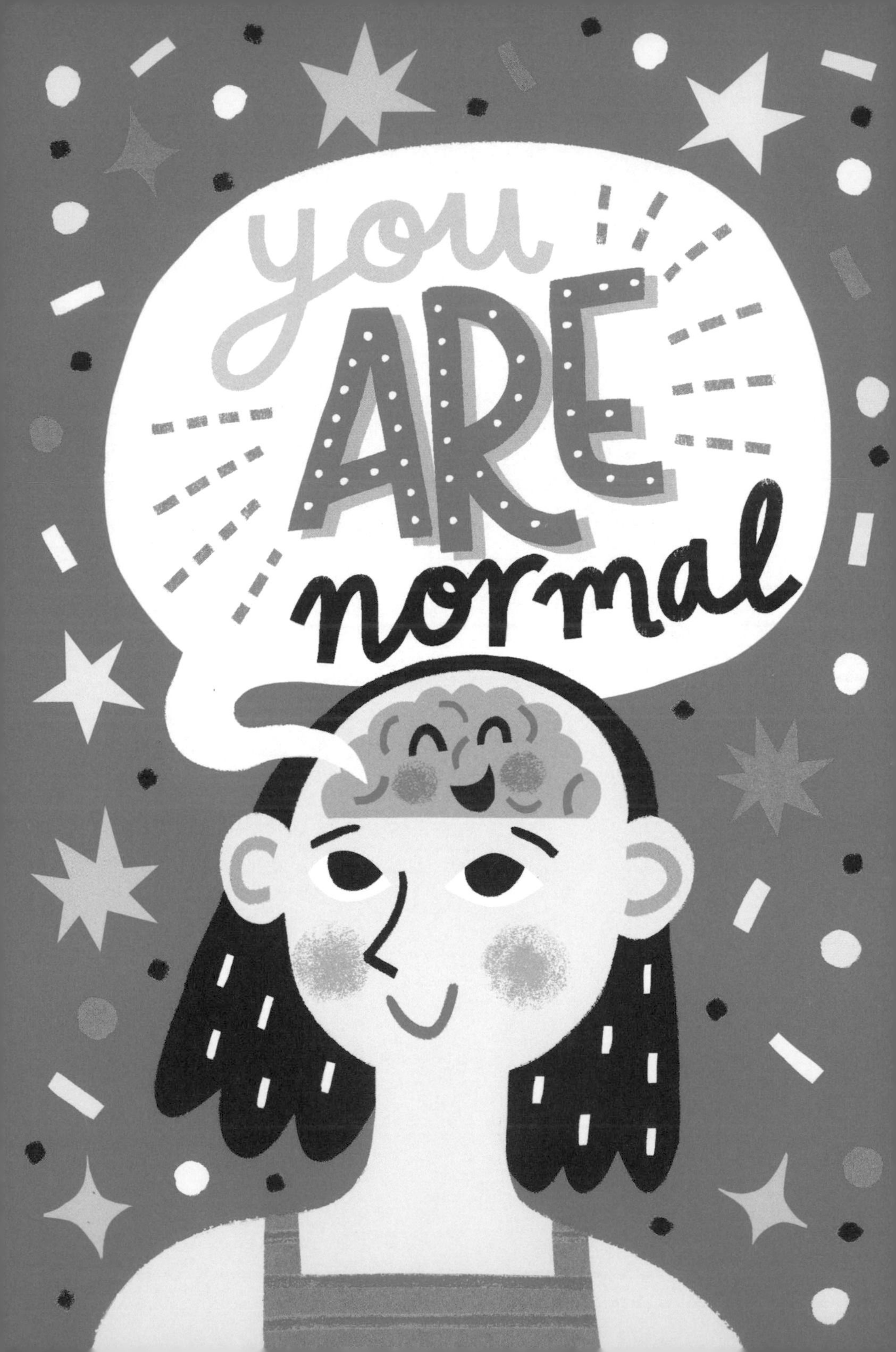
you
ARE
normal

Eight

- Fitting in and keeping up with your mates can feel hard at times. Never feel you have to be anything you're not. You are your own brilliantly unique person.

- Talking really is the best way of getting any rubbish feelings off your chest and out of your head. If you're struggling to speak out loud, explore other ways of offloading, such as writing an email, letter, story or poem, or singing.

- Help is out there! Family and friends, your school counsellor or favourite teacher, the family doctor, a helpline... Never feel silly or embarrassed to ask for help.

You've reached the final chapter! Well done for sticking with the book all the way through. I hope you're feeling a lot more clued up and empowered about your own mental health – what makes you tick, and most importantly, what doesn't. This chapter is where we bring together all the stuff we've learned and focus on who you are and what's great about you. Putting number one (that's you!) first is key in making sure you feel physically, mentally and emotionally well.

Of course, we must think of others and be kind and thoughtful at all times – being completely selfish isn't the nicest thing.

But, being a little bit selfish when it comes to your own health and feelings is okay.

In fact, it helps to make sure you're listening to your own needs.

Perhaps you find hanging out with certain mates draining at times ... maybe home life is hectic and you could do with some space ... perhaps school gets too much and you could use a bit of slack from teachers and parents. The best way to make sure you're heard on all of these things – surprise, surprise – is to talk! It sounds obvious, but talking can be the hardest thing to do.

You might be like me and burst into tears every time you try to say how you feel, and then get annoyed with yourself for crying. DON'T! **Talking and speaking about your feelings is 100 per cent brave and seriously mature**. It doesn't mean you are weak – in fact, the opposite.

A good (cry) is one of the best ways to get all the negative tension, stress and any anxiety out.

Trust me – it's way better to have it out of your head than festering away inside.

Knowing what you want and need to do to stay on top of your mental health is a big part of being your own boss. In a world where we're always connected, where social media tells us that we must look/sound/be a certain way, we run the risk of forgetting who we are, what we are great at, our talents, what we're proud of. We forget to celebrate our own unique individuality – **no filter!**

LOVE YOURSELF!

Let's get some self-appreciation going on. I mean, if we don't love ourselves, even a tiny bit, how can we expect others to love us, right?

On a piece of paper, or a tablet, chalkboard, journal, sticky note – whatever! – write:

THIS IS ME!

Now, this is where you're going to get creative. List all the fab, unique, interesting things about you. The stuff about you that makes you proud. Here's my list as an example:

Anna's This is Me!

- I'm a kind and loyal friend
- I can cook a really good spaghetti Bolognese
- I'm a pretty good singer
- I help my nanna and keep her company when she's lonely
- I smile at people when they're sad to make them feel happier
- I help charities and people less fortunate than myself

You can make your list as long as you like. And keep adding to it every time you do something that makes you feel proud.

Read your list back to yourself out loud, **and feel good about who you are**. When we feel good about ourselves, our confidence and self-esteem tends to improve. And when this happens, all the feel-good happy chemicals in your brain bubble away nicely, giving your mental and emotional health a big tick.

YES OR NO?

I used to be a 'people pleaser' – I would say 'yes' to everyone and everything because I didn't want to let people down or have anyone think bad thoughts about me. Sounds like a nice way to be, I guess ... but actually it's not, if saying 'yes' means that you're putting your own happiness at the bottom of the list.

That's what happened with me. I was so busy saying 'yes' to this party and 'yes' to that mate that there wasn't any time left for me. I ended up tired, cranky, anxious, worried and feeling like I'd said 'yes' to so much stuff that I wasn't doing anything properly.

So, heads-up, buddy – have a think about what (and who) you're saying 'yes' to in your life. It's great to be a good pal! But always ask yourself these questions:

- Who am I doing this for?
- Have I got the time and energy to do it properly?

- Am I being kind to my mental health?

Always try to be guided by what your inner voice says back. Put your own limits in place and keep checking in with your mood and feelings. This way you can work out what you want to say 'yes' to, but also importantly when it's in your best interest to say 'no'. That way you've been super clear and if anyone gets annoyed, it's their problem.

HOW TO SAY NO!

Saying 'no' can be really hard, particularly if you're a 'yes' person and worry about upsetting someone! Remember, if keeping yourself happy and well means saying 'no', then so be it.

Try experimenting with different ways to say 'no':

I can't do that now, but I'll let you know when I can.

It's not for me.

I'll let you know.

GIVE IT A TRY.

ONLINE AND *In Real Life*

We can never talk enough about being clued-up about online life. Social media is a massive part of life, and as it's a fairly recent thing, adults and parents struggle to accept and understand it.

The online world is a huge place and there's so much that's great about it – shopping, gaming, chatting to mates, watching YouTube videos, and so on. But there's also a darker side, which you'll be aware of through your school safety guidelines, and which we need to bear in mind at all times in order to keep safe and well, both physically and mentally. Some of the more worrying aspects of being online include:

CYBERBULLYING
When electronic devices are used to send upsetting or hurtful messages.

PORN
Online images of a sexual nature.

SEXTING
The sending, forwarding or receiving of sexually explicit messages, photos or videos.

When an adult attempts to make friends with a child with  the intention of sexual abuse.

BODY-SHAMING
When unkind comments are made or someone is humiliated because of the way they look.

ONLINE SAFETY TIPS

Never ever give out your personal details – for example, your address, phone number, bank account details.

Change your passwords regularly to ensure your online security is top notch.

Report anything suspicious or that makes you feel uncomfortable straight away. Tell a parent or trusted adult, block the dodgy follower or friend, and report what has happened to the app or website provider.

Never agree to meet someone alone who you've only met online. They may not be who they say they are.

A good way of remembering what's okay to post or share online is to ask yourself, 'Would I be happy if my Gran saw this?' If the answer is no, then don't post it. Once you've hit 'post' or 'share', it's out of your hands forever and in cyberspace for good.

Remember your digital footprint – everything you post online is permanent and could come back to haunt you in the future.

Although it may be fun to let your friends know where you are, keep your location private! Turn off location tracking on your phone for ultimate privacy.

HEADS-UP!

Over **93 million selfies** are taken around the world every single day. Some of the most followed social media 'stars' spend hours posing, filtering and uploading the 'perfect' selfie.

What we don't see are the millions of photos that didn't make it online – the less than perfect ones. Social media **should not be taken seriously**. So, the next time you feel you need to look more like your fave Instagram celeb, remember 'that post' is often the work of clever posing, filters, apps and people who are paid to make it look like that.

TALKING IT OUT

Throughout this book I've made a point about the **importance of talking**. The reason I'm such a fan of talking to someone you trust about your feelings and what's going on in your head is because I've been in the situation where I didn't do that. I kept all my worries and scary thoughts to myself. I was too embarrassed to tell anyone how I was feeling, and I didn't really understand what I was feeling either. I just felt lonely, scared and very, very anxious.

Eventually, all my feelings and anxiety bubbled over and **I had to ask for help.** And the help I got from my doctors, parents and friends was brilliant ... so brilliant that I instantly wished I'd asked for it sooner! There wasn't a 'magic formula' that made it all okay again, but just telling people how I was feeling and allowing others to support me really was the biggest thing that helped me to feel better and get through it.

If you do decide to speak to someone, think about what you want to say and choose a convenient time to do it.

It can be hard to find the right words so you might like to practise first – try talking to yourself in the mirror or even telling the dog! If you find talking out loud difficult, you can write down what you want to say and either read it out loud or give it to the person you want to talk to. (There's a letter template on page 174.)

The Professionals

Doctors

Lots of people think that doctors are scary, but let's remember that they are just regular human beings! A doctor should always make you feel respected and listen confidentially without judging you (what you say stays between you and the doctor). You can visit your doctor at any age about anything to do with physical and mental health. You have a right to see a doctor by yourself, but going with an adult or even a friend can really help you feel supported.

Counsellors

Counsellors, or therapists, are people specifically trained

to listen and help you find ways of dealing with emotional and personal issues. Finding the right counsellor is quite a personal thing. A doctor can refer you to a counsellor for therapy, and it's a good idea to chat to your parents to ask for their support, too. You can also find and talk to a counsellor yourself – look at the back of the book for where to go for help.

MYTH BUSTING

'Counselling isn't confidential.'

BUSTED!

Yes, counsellors are professionals in what they do, it is a safe space to talk and they do not judge you. They might ask you questions about your life, your family, how you're feeling and about any worries or concerns you might have. Anything you tell them will be confidential (which means they won't tell anyone without your permission). There are only a few times when a counsellor might need to tell another professional, such as if you're in danger, but they will always discuss it with you first.

Medication

Sometimes medicine might be suggested and monitored by a specialist mental health doctor (a psychiatrist). Medication, such as antidepressants, isn't usually suggested for people under the age of eighteen due to possible side effects, but there are situations when it might be helpful, particularly if talking therapy isn't working. Prescription medication must always be taken seriously and it's not to be messed about with.

Mental Health: Sorted. Well done!

To Sum It All Up...

Mental health can be so misunderstood, but it shouldn't be feared and you should never feel ashamed or embarrassed about yours.

Keep strong, my friend, and remember – *you* are the boss of your mental health.

Anna x

Letter Template

To_____

Today I feel _____

Recently, I have been feeling_____

I would like_____

What I don't need is _____

It's really unhelpful when _____

I would love it if _____

I would like us to _____

What I need from you right now is _____

You can help me best by _____

What's next – please can you _____

I would/wouldn't like to talk further

_____

You can best communicate back to me by

_____

From _____